PowerPoint for Windows explained

OTHER TITLES OF INTEREST

PowerPoint for Windows explained

By

David Weale

BERNARD BABANI (publishing) LTD
THE GRAMPIANS
SHEPHERDS BUSH ROAD
LONDON W6 7NF
ENGLAND

PLEASE NOTE

Although every care has been taken with the production of this book to ensure that any instructions or any of the other contents operate in a correct and safe manner, the Author and the Publishers do not accept any responsibility for any failure, damage or loss caused by following the said contents. The Author and Publisher do not take any responsibility for errors or omissions.

The Author and Publisher will not be liable to the purchaser or to any other person or legal entity with respect to any liability, loss or damage (whether direct, indirect, special, incidental or consequential) caused or alleged to be caused directly or indirectly by this book.

The book is sold as is, without any warranty of any kind, either expressed or implied, respecting the contents, including but not limited to implied warranties regarding the book's quality, performance, correctness or fitness for any particular purpose.

No part of this book may be reproduced or copied by any means whatever without written permission of the Publisher.

© 1995 BERNARD BABANI (publishing) LTD
Screen Shot(s) reprinted with permission from Microsoft Corporation.

First published - October 1995

British Library Cataloguing in Publication Data

Weale. D
Powerpoint for Windows Explained
I.Title
006.6869

ISBN 0 85934 389 8

Cover design by Gregor Arthur
Cover illustration by Adam Willis
Printed and bound in Great Britain by Cox & Wyman Ltd., Reading.

ABOUT THE AUTHOR

David Weale is a Fellow of the Institute of Chartered Accountants and has worked in both private and public practice. He is a lecturer in business computing at Yeovil College.

He is the author of several books on computing and lives in Somerset with his wife, three children and Siamese cat.

DEDICATION

I had fun writing this book and would hope that you, the reader, have fun reading it. This dedication is for you, the reader.

TRADEMARKS

Preface

Welcome to this book, I wrote it as an alternative to the manual to explain the program in a way which looks at how to produce and enhance your own presentations.

I have used Powerpoint to create my own slide shows and presentations for some years and have found it an excellent program. The latest version (v.4) contains all the strengths of the previous version together with some super additional features.

Each chapter of the book covers a specific aspect of the program and contains various hints and techniques that I have found useful in my own work and which may not be obvious.

This text has been written both with the new user in mind and for the more experienced person as it contains explanations of the more technical and sophisticated features

Please note that I anticipate that you understand the basic techniques of using Windows itself. If you do not then there are many excellent texts on the market.

I hope you learn from this book and have as much enjoyment using the program as I do.

David Weale, October 1995

Contents

Introduction

When you load Microsoft® PowerPoint™ you will see the screen shown below.

> **Hint:**
> ☐ This screen can be customised (setup) as you want and what you see here is the default layout

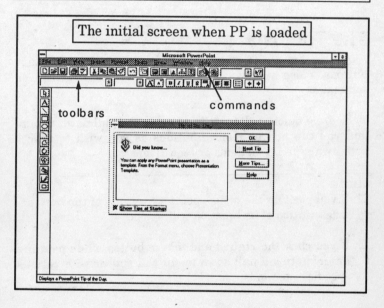

The initial screen when PP is loaded

toolbars

commands

The Pull Down Menus

Along the top of the screen are the commands. When you click the mouse pointer on any of these, a pull down menu will appear. These contain several related commands (some of which can also be carried out using the toolbar buttons).

Hint:
☐ Use the left hand mouse button except where told to use the right hand button.

The Toolbars

Along the top of the screen are two toolbars, these contain buttons which you can click on to carry out activities or commands.

They are a quicker alternative to using the pull down menus and you can add or remove buttons as you wish to reflect your own especial methods or requirements.

Hints:
☐ If you position the mouse pointer over any of the buttons, a description of its function will appear.

☐ If you click the **right** hand mouse button while pointing at any button a pull down menu will appear with various specific commands.

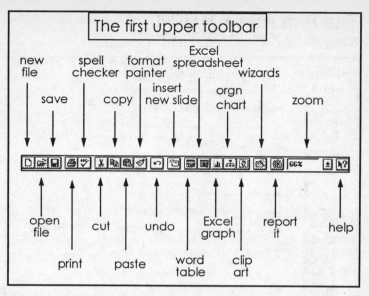

The first upper toolbar

new file
save
spell checker
format painter
copy
insert new slide
Excel spreadsheet
orgn chart
wizards
zoom

open file
print
cut
paste
undo
word table
Excel graph
clip art
report it
help

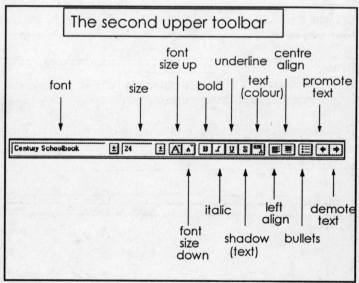

The second upper toolbar

font
size
font size up
bold
underline
text (colour)
centre align
promote text

font size down
italic
shadow (text)
left align
bullets
demote text

Century Schoolbook   24

The Drawing Toolbar is to the left of the screen and at the bottom of the screen is a further toolbar

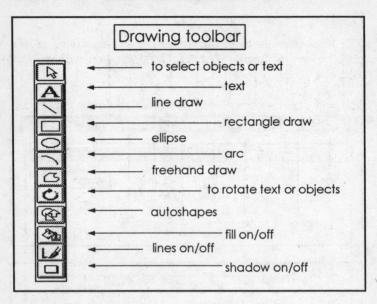

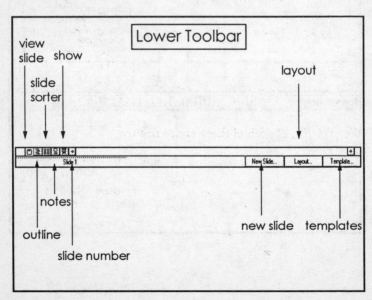

4

Automating Your Work

The next stage is to begin creating a presentation. After clicking on OK for the **Tip Of The Day**, you will see the following dialog box.

You will also see this dialog box when you open a new file (**File** and then **New**).

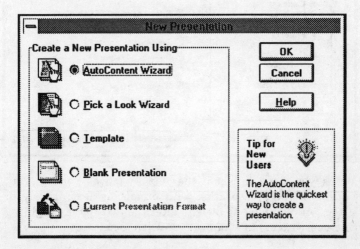

This gives you a choice of how you want to create your presentation.

We will look at each of these styles in turn.

Auto Content Wizard

This is a step-through set of screens which ask you to enter certain information, the third screen is shown below to illustrate the range of types of presentation the Wizard can produce.

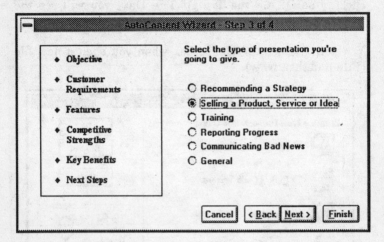

When you have finished, the Wizard leaves you with an outline of the presentation with prompting text already in place. All you have to do is to alter the text (by highlighting and overwriting) to whatever you wish to say.

An example of an outline is shown below.

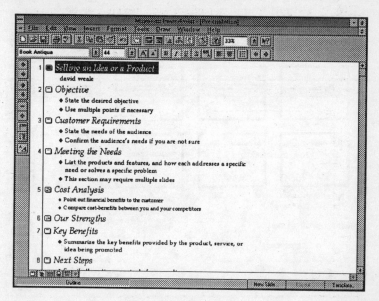

When you have finished you can look at all the slides by clicking on the **Slide Sorter** button along the bottom of the screen.

You will see the following display.

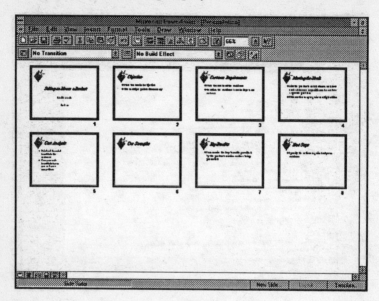

If you want to look at each slide in turn then you need to click on the **Slide View** button (again along the bottom of the screen) to make the slides full screen.

The initial slide may look similar to this.

You can move from slide to slide by clicking on the double-arrowed buttons (on the bottom right of the screen)

Finally you can view the slide show as it would appear on an OHP or projected onto a screen by clicking on the **Show** button along the bottom of the screen.

Hint:
☐ When you view a slide show make sure you are at the start of the file.

Pick a Look Wizard

This is a quick method of obtaining the framework for your slides.

You will be taken through a series of nine dialog boxes, each requesting you to choose between various types of layout and to enter certain information you want to appear on each slide.

This differs from the **Auto Content Wizard**, you are choosing your layout, there is no text entered for you apart from information that is common to all the slides such as your name.

On some of the dialog boxes you can make certain choices by clicking on the different items and immediately see the result previewed for you, for example the third dialog box lets you choose a template from a list and you can see how each looks by clicking on the name.

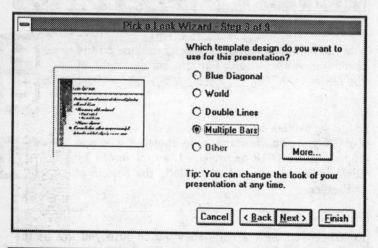

Hint:

☐ On some dialog boxes (such as the one shown above) there is a **More** button, clicking on this gives you a greater choice of items.

The fourth dialog box is shown to illustrate the different types of ways you can output your presentation.

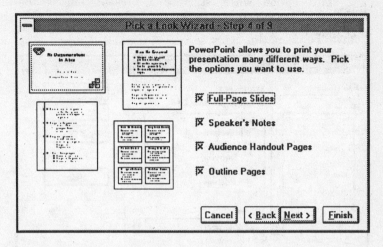

Finally the initial slide will be displayed and you can begin to create your presentation by entering the text.

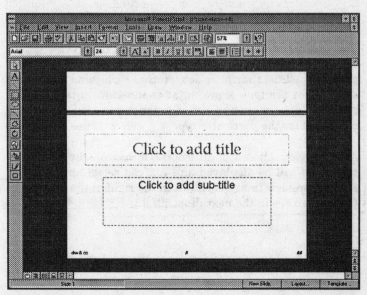

Template

The third option when starting a presentation is the template. After selecting this, the first screen you will see is that shown below.

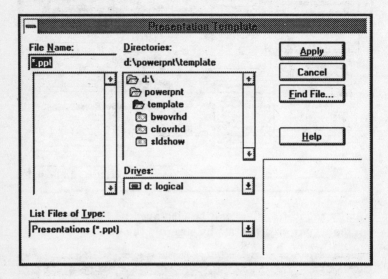

You can choose between three directories, **bwovrhd** (black & white overheads), **clrovrhd** (colour overheads) and **sldshow** (slide show). Each of these contains templates suitable for the type of presentation needed. In fact most of the templates in each of the directories are similar but are optimised for the particular type, e.g. colour slides.

After having chosen a directory, a list of the available templates will be displayed and you can select any of these. A small preview image is shown in the right of the dialog box (as you can see in the next illustration).

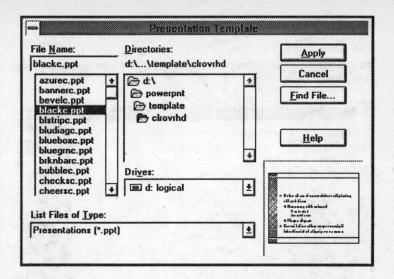

Having chosen a template you will see the **Layout** dialog box. This is where you can select a layout for your presentation from those displayed.

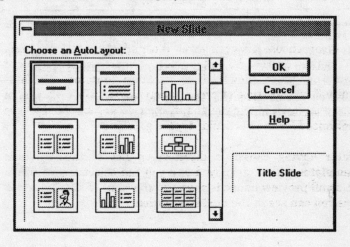

Finally the first slide in your new presentation will appear on the screen.

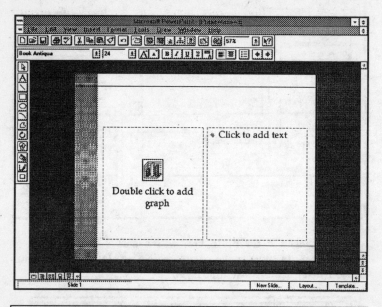

Hints:

☐ To alter the layout, click on the **Layout** button along the bottom of the screen and select an alternative layout.

☐ You can click on the **Template** button along the bottom of the screen to alter the template.

Blank Presentation

The fourth choice of new presentation is the blank presentation. This merely gives you a choice of layout without the addition of a template. The only dialog box is shown below.

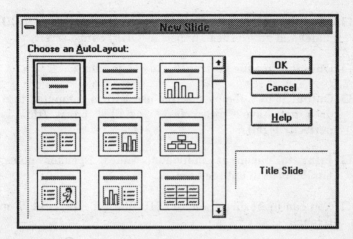

This is an ideal choice if you wish to apply a template at a later stage.

> **Hint:**
> ☐ When you apply a template it may alter the layout of headings and may also use a different font. It is worthwhile selecting a template early on.

Current Presentation Format

This will start a new presentation with the same format (including template) as the current one that is displayed at that time. You will, however, be given the opportunity to alter the layout.

You will only be able to select this option if there is a presentation already open.

Output

You can output your presentation slides in various ways.

☐ As a slide show either on the screen or using an LCD panel and an overhead projector (OHP) onto a screen.

☐ Output it to a file for transfer to 35mm film.

☐ Output it to a floppy disc for use with a computer that does not have PowerPoint™ installed on it (this is perfectly legal).

☐ Print to paper as individual slides, speaker notes, handouts or in outline form.

☐ You can print directly onto OHP film (in either B&W or colour).

Slide Shows

This is the usual way of presenting and you can build in special effects such as **Transitions** and **Builds**.

Make sure you are at the start of the slides and then click on the **Slide Show** button along the bottom of the screen

Your slides will then appear one after the other on the screen.

To advance to the next slide click the left hand mouse button.

> **Hint:**
> ☐ To go backwards use the right-hand mouse button.

Transitions

This is a special effect between each slide, to use this select the **Tools** menu and then **Transition**.

The dialog box will appear and as you select from the various options you can preview the effect in the right hand side of the box.

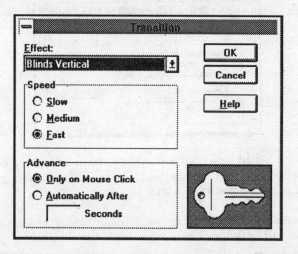

Hint:

□ To create a running display select the **Automatically After Seconds** box and enter the number of seconds you want each slide displayed for. This is ideal for exhibitions, etc.

Builds

Whereas Transitions work between slides, **Builds** literally build a slide up point by point. **Builds** can be applied to all the slides or to any you select.

Again use the **Tools** menu and this time select **Build**.

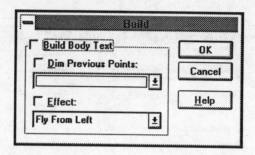

Click on **Build Body Text** and then you can alter the colour that the previous points will be in, you can also change the effect of each point as it is built.

The latest point will be in the primary colour, the previous points will be dimmed to the colour of your choice.

Hiding Slides

You can hide slides (within a presentation file) so that they do not display. This may be useful for certain audiences.

You can hide the current slide or if you are in **Slide Sorter View** you can select several slides.

Hint:
☐ Remember that if you want to select several slides hold down the **Shift** key while clicking the mouse pointer on each.

To hide a slide use the **Tools** menu and then **Hide Slide** or if you are in **Slide Sorter View** you can use the **Hide Slide** button (on the upper toolbar).

Displaying Hidden Slides

Either type the character **H** while displaying the previous slide or click on the hidden slide button (displayed on the previous slide during a slide show, you may need to move the mouse to display it).

Adding Freehand Drawing to a Slide Show

Another button shown only during slide shows is the freehand draw symbol. If you click on this you can add freehand drawings or lines to a slide while it is being displayed.

You need to click on the symbol again to change the mouse pointer back to an arrow to move onto the next slide. You may also use the ESC key do this.

Branching to Another Slide Show

Occasionally while carrying out a presentation you may want to open another set of slides, display them and then return to the original slide show at the same place you left it.

To do this, make sure you are in **Slide View** (a single slide is displayed on the screen) and then using the **Insert** menu choose **Object** and then **PowerPoint™ Presentation**.

Click on the **Create from File** option and enter the filename.

The new file will show as an object within the slide it branches from.

Finally use the **Tools** menu to select **Play Settings** (see below) and choose your options from this.

Hint:
☐ You can have numerous branches from one slide show.

Play Settings

This option is only available when the inserted object or slide is selected and lets you determine how the branched item is displayed

For example choosing **When Transition** means that the branched set of slides will be displayed when the transition is made to the next slide.

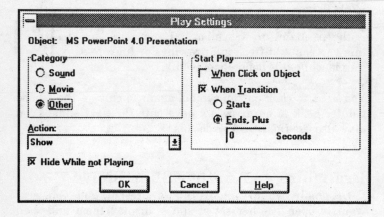

Output to a File for Transfer to 35mm Film

This is a fairly specialised activity and the file would have to be sent to a special laboratory. What follows is a general overview, you should contact the firm carrying out the transfer to check exactly what they require.

Pull down the **File** menu and choose **Print**. A dialog box will appear.

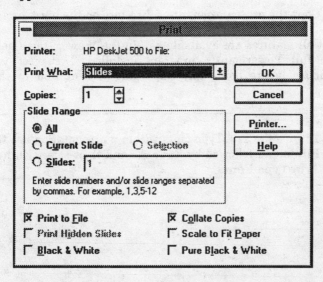

Select **Print to File** and you will be asked for a file name.

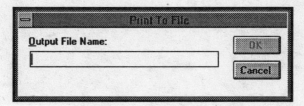

Using other Computers

This is very useful, especially if you are giving a presentation somewhere else and are unsure that they have PowerPoint™. To do this carry out the following:

☐ Make a copy of the original **Viewer** disk.

☐ Copy your presentation onto another disc.

☐ Run Vsetup.Exe.

☐ Copy the presentation into a directory on the hard disc.

Not all features are available within the Viewer, some need the full PowerPoint™ program installed, I suggest you practise before doing any important presentation in this way.

Hint:
☐ To save the TrueType fonts within a presentation use the **File** menu followed by **Save As** and then select **Embed TrueType Fonts**.

Printing onto Paper

To print your file click on the **print** button along the upper toolbar.

A dialog box will be displayed.

This shows that the file is being printed to the default printer.

Hints:
☐ If you have several printers then you can select the one you want by clicking on the **File** command along the top of the screen and then select **Print**. This displays a dialog box from which you can click on **Printer** to alter the printer.

Using this dialog box you can also choose various other parameters, for example the number of copies you want to print. The dialog box is shown on the next page.

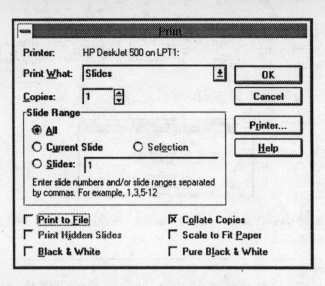

As you can see there are several options, some need an explanation.

Print What
You can output the file as :

☐ Individual slides (one to a page).

☐ Notes pages (you can type notes on the page as well as display the slide).

☐ Handouts (2, 3 or 6 slides per page).

☐ Outline pages.

Print to File
This has been covered in the section on 35mm slides.

Print Hidden Files

You can hide certain slides within your presentation and only show them if you wish, selecting this option will include them in the printout.

Black & White

This makes all colour fills into B&W and borders all unbordered objects.

Collate Copies

Collates the copies.

Scale to Fit Paper

Alters the scale to fit the paper size being used.

Pure Black & White

Makes everything B&W or grey scale.

Making OHP slides

This follows the same pattern as printing to paper.

Hint:
☐ Make sure you use the correct OHP film in your printer otherwise the results could be interesting and/or expensive.

Viewing Your Slides

There are several different ways of looking at the slides.

☐ Slides

☐ Outline

☐ Slide Sorter

☐ Notes Pages

☐ Slide Show

Slides

This is the default (the normal way the slides are displayed). Each slide is shown full screen and you can move from slide to slide by using the buttons on the right of the screen.

Note that you can alter the size of the display either by clicking on the **Zoom Control** button on the upper toolbar or by pulling down the **View** menu and choosing **Zoom**.

The **Zoom** menu is shown below, you can choose a percentage or enter a figure as you choose.

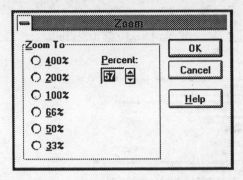

Outline

Only the titles and main text of all your slides are shown, each slide is numbered and they are shown in sequence.

Outline has two major uses :

☐ Being able to see all the main text in this way lets you alter the formatting and rearrange it.

☐ You can import outlines from other programs, such as Word™ 6 which lets you use the **Report It** button on the toolbar to import directly.

Outline View screens look like this.

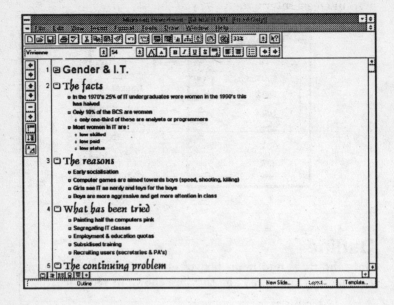

Note the new buttons that appear in Outline, they are explained below.

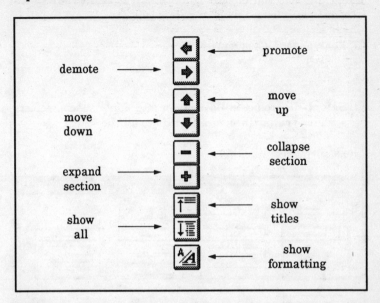

Report It

This button on the toolbar enables you to edit outlines within Word™ which is more flexible than editing them directly within PowerPoint™.

Slide Sorter

Using this lets you display (small) images of all your slides in sequence. Using this feature lets you:

☐ Rearrange the sequence.

or

☐ **Select All** from the **Edit** menu and apply special effects such as **Transitions** and **Builds** to all the slides.

The screen looks like this :

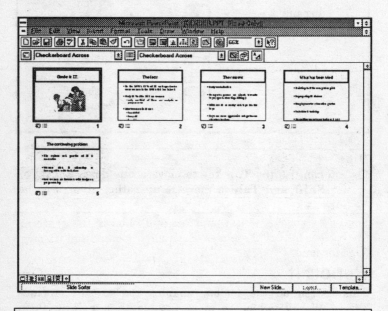

Hint:
☐ To alter the size of the slides use the **Zoom** button.

To move the slides around, simply click on a slide with the mouse and then drag it to a new position (between two slides). The other slides will rearrange themselves.

Notes Page

Useful for the person actually doing the presentation. This lets you add text notes to a page which contains a slide in the top half .

The screen looks like this :

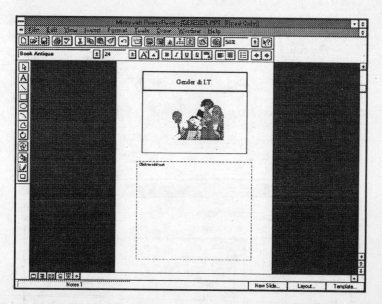

You add your own text, comments and so on in the space in the bottom half of the page. Each slide is allocated its own page for notes

Slide Show

This was dealt with in the chapter on **Output**.

File Handling

Saving Your Work

You should get in the habit of saving your work regularly so that any problems whether hardware or software do not cause too much loss of time or other problems.

To save your work you can click on the **save** button which is on the toolbar along the top of the screen.

The first time you save your file, you will see a dialog box asking for a file name.

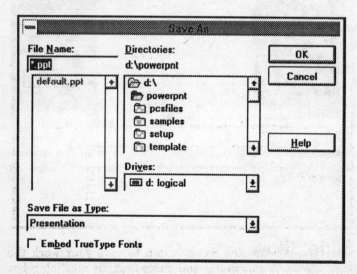

At this point you can change the **drive** or **directory** to which you want to save.

The file name can be up to eight characters, you must not use full stops or special characters, it is best to restrict yourself to letters and numbers.

The program will automatically add a full stop and an extension **PPT** to the file name and after you have finished saving, this will appear along the top of the screen.

You will then see another dialog box (this only appears when you first save a file or change the name under which it is saved).

This is the **Summary Info** box and lets you add information about the presentation.

Hint:
☐ If you find this irritating, you can turn this box off by using the **Tools** and **Options** menu and turning off the selection for **Prompt for Summary Info**.

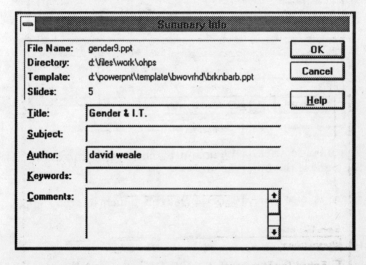

Next time you use the **Save** button to save your work the process will be automatic and there will be no dialog box appearing.

Hint:
☐ If you want to change the drive or directory or change the name of the file then click on the **File** command along the top of the screen and then on **Save As**.

Find File

This option within the **File** menu lets you find your lost files and see what is contained within each file. It is an option available within all mainstream Microsoft products and can be extremely useful.

The dialog box within PowerPoint™ looks like this.

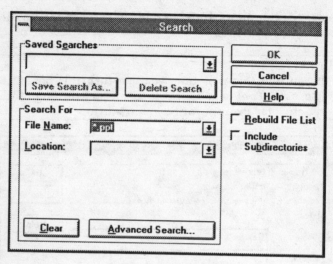

You have to select a **Location** by clicking on the arrow to the right of the Location box.

There is also an **Advanced Search** which lets you make various choices.

Hint:
☐ Make sure you click on the **Include Subdirectories** button otherwise you may not find any files.

After clicking on the OK button you will see a display similar to that shown.

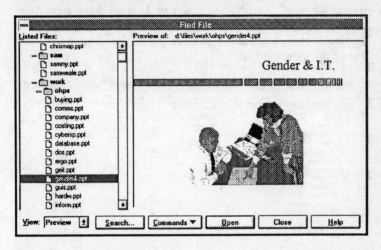

You will only be able to preview certain slides, for example you cannot preview PowerPoint™ v.3 slides until they have been converted to v.4.

Along the bottom of the **File Find** dialog box you can see the following series of buttons.

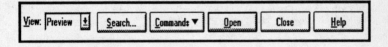

View

You can see a **Preview** of the slides within that file (the initial slide of the file), or you can look at **File Info** (see below) which is similar to the **Windows File Manager**, or you can view **Summary** which gives the Summary Info about the selected file.

File Name	Title	Size	Author	Last Saved
⊞ d:	- drive -			
⊞ files	- directory -			
⊞ chris	- directory -			
chrismap.ppt		25K		Apr 03, 1995
⊞ sam	- directory -			
sammy.ppt		10K		Jan 18, 1994
samweale.ppt		11K		Jan 18, 1994
⊞ work	- directory -			
⊞ ohps	- directory -			
buying.ppt		65K		Oct 24, 1994
comms.ppt		20K		Jan 16, 1995
company.ppt		14K		Mar 13, 1994
costing.ppt		355K		Feb 07, 1995
cybersp.ppt		59K		Jan 22, 1995
database.ppt		45K		Oct 29, 1994
dos.ppt		18K		Jan 15, 1994
ergo.ppt		44K		Feb 07, 1995
geit.ppt		28K		Mar 29, 1995
gender4.ppt	Gender 4-1-1	83K	david weale	Mar 19, 1995

View: File Info | Search... | Commands ▼ | Open | Cancel | Help

Search

This reverts to the original screen so that you can alter the search parameters.

Commands

Open Read Only
Print...
Summary...
Delete
Copy...
Sorting...

This pulls down a menu which lets you open the file **Read Only** which means that if you want to alter it you will have to save the altered version under another name.

You can also print the file, display summary information about the file, delete the file or copy it. Finally you can sort the files into different orders (within their directory structure).

Open/Cancel/Help
These are self explanatory.

Summary Info

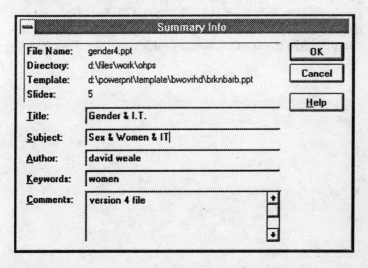

This dialog box appears when you save a file for the first time and you can recall it and amend it by using the **File** and **Summary Info** commands. You can enter any useful information

Altering the Default Setup

Any permanent changes you want to make to the original default settings can be saved in the DEFAULT.PPT file which is loaded when you begin the program. Simply make the changes and save the file as DEFAULT.PPT which is normally in the main PowerPoint™ directory.

Converting from Other Programs

This should be an automatic activity (provided the correct filters and conversion programs were installed). PowerPoint™ will load them as **Read-Only** which means that you will not be able to make changes to the original file but will have to save the changes under another file name.

Text

In this chapter you will be looking at the various ways of entering and manipulating text within your presentation.

Entering Text

This is simple, just click where you are prompted and type the text.

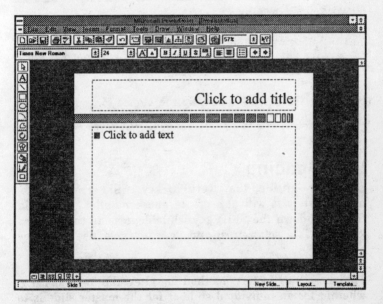

To move on to the next point, use the **return** key and a new bullet will appear below the original.

Altering the Font

Each template has a font allocated to it, often this is ideal, but if you want to alter the font then there are two methods.

☐ Highlight the text and then click on the **Font** button along the upper toolbar and choose another font. You can also alter the **Font Size**.

☐ Alter the **Master Slide** so that all the text within all the slides in the current file changes to the new font/font size (see section on master slides)

Hints:
☐ To select all the text just click inside the text to bring up the text border, making sure that there are small black squares shown around the border (you may need to click on the border to show these).

☐ Alternatively click and drag the mouse to highlight and select the text.

Line Spacing

Obviously hitting the **Return** key will create space, unfortunately it will also create another bullet. To avoid this, hold down the **Shift** key while depressing the **Return** key, this is a soft return and does not give rise to a new bullet.

The most satisfactory method to alter the line spacing, whether for an individual slide or for the master slide is to use the **Format** command (along the top of the screen) and then **Line Spacing**.

A dialog box will appear and you can alter the line spacing and the space before and after paragraphs as you wish. Better still you will be able to see the effect on screen as you make the changes.

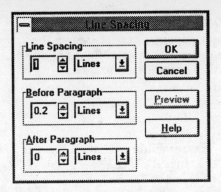

Hint:
□ Grab the dialog box and move it out of the way so that you can see the effect more clearly.

Altering the Alignment of the Text

To alter the alignment of a paragraph (or more), highlight the text and then either pull down the **Format** menu and select **Alignment** or use the alignment buttons on the toolbar.

Hint:
□ The Alignment menu gives more choice (you can align to the right or justify the text, the buttons only enable you to align left or centre).

Alternatively you can use the following keys (holding the first down while depressing the latter).

CTRL E	centre
CTRL J	justify
CTRL L	left
CTRL R	right

Hint:
☐ To line up columns of text or figures use the tab key, do NOT use the spacebar as while it might look lined up on screen it may not print out properly.

Changing Case

A new feature of version 4 is being able to change the case of the text you have typed in. Believe me this is very useful, it is only too easy to type text with the **Caps Lock** key on by mistake.

To use this feature you need to highlight the text and then pull down the **Format** menu and select **Change Case**. Then choose how you want to alter the text.

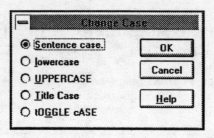

Find

A standard text tool, this enables you to find words or parts of words within your presentation.

The dialog box is shown below.

You enter the word or phrase you are looking for and click on the **Match Case** and/or **Find Whole Words Only** if this is what you wish.

Click on the **Find Next** button and the first occurrence of the word will be found and then you can move to the next by clicking on the **Find Next** button and so on.

Hint:
☐ You can close down the dialog box and use **Shift** and **F4** to repeat the search.

Replace

Very similar to **Find** except you choose to replace the word or phrase with another as you can see from the dialog box.

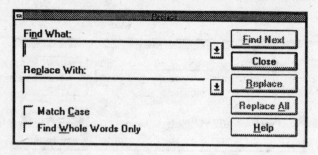

Periods

This is an *Americanism* for full stops and enables you to add or remove full stops from selected text. This is a wonderful way to maintain consistency in your slides.

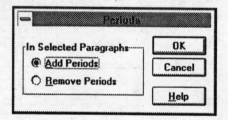

Changing the Bullets

If you want to alter the predefined bullets (again you can make these changes for an individual slide or for all the slides by altering the master slide), firstly select the text for which you want to alter the bullets and then pull down the **Format** menu and select **Bullets**.

There are various options. You can choose bullets from any character set you have installed and you can alter the colour of the bullet and/or its relative size.

You can remove bullets by clicking on the **Use a Bullet** box so that there is not an X in it (after selecting the text).

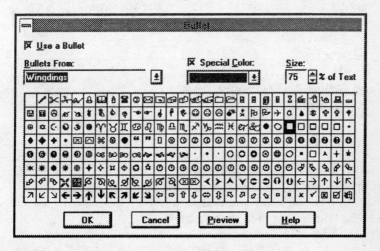

Changing the Text Colour

Although a template will automatically use its own colour scheme, you can alter the text colour easily.

This can be done in two ways.

☐ Select the text to be changed by clicking within the text area so that the text box appears around the text. Then either click on the **Format** menu and then **Font**, then click on the **Colour** box and select a different colour.

Or

☐ After selecting the text, click on the **Change Colour** button on the toolbar and alter the colour.

Hint:
☐ You can highlight any character or characters and alter its colour irrespective of the remainder of the text.

Changing Fonts

Within the **Tools** menu is an option called **Replace Fonts**. This lets you alter one font to another, so that all type in that font is altered to the new font.

The dialog box is shown below, you can use the arrows to the right of each box to alter the choices.

Text Anchor

After selecting the text, pull down the **Format** menu and then **Text Anchor**; the following dialog box will be shown.

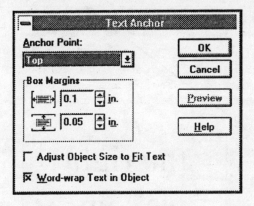

You can alter the anchor point itself and the margins for the text to give different effects to selected text.

Below are two illustrations, a before and after, the after example has had the left and right margins made larger.

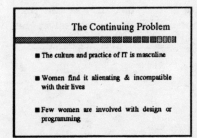

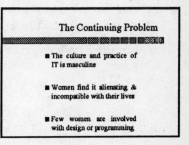

This technique can also be used to fit text within a shape as shown below.

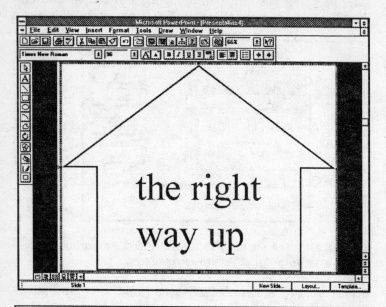

Hint:
☐ You do **not** have to create a text box or use the text button to add text to a shape or object. Simply select the object and begin typing.

Rotating Text

As well as being able to rotate objects, PowerPoint™ v.4 enables you to rotate text.

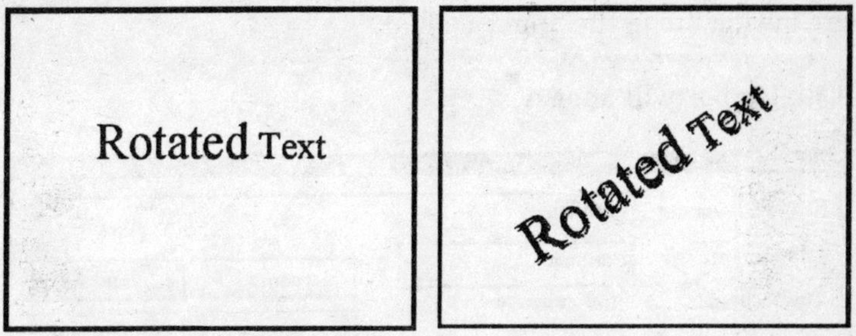

Rotated Text	*Rotated Text* (rotated diagonally)

To do this simply select the text and use the **Draw** menu and then **Rotate/Flip**. You can see the effect in the illustration where the text has also been shadowed.

Spell Checking Your Text

It is very easy to destroy a presentation by using incorrect spelling. PowerPoint™ includes a spell checker which is accessed by clicking on the button along the upper toolbar.

A dialog box will appear.

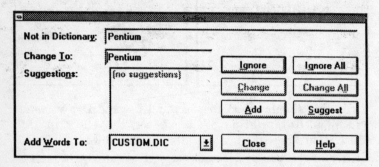

As you can see there are various buttons which you can use.

Hint:
☐ Use the **Custom Dictionary** to add specialist words you use but which are not in the main dictionary.

The way a spell checker operates is to compare every word you enter against a (finite) list of words. If the word you type is not in the list the spell checker program will identify it. This does **not** mean it is wrong, merely that it is not in the dictionary.

Adding Graphics & Objects

It is always useful and rewarding to add some form of visuals to your presentation. You can add

☐ Clipart (from the library that comes with the program)

☐ Pictures or scanned images

☐ A Word for Windows™ table

☐ Graphs

☐ WordArt™ or any other object such as an equation or a drawing you have make within Paintbrush™ or a chart from Excel™ or Works™

☐ Organisation Charts

Clipart

Select the slide you want to add the image to (use the scroll bars on the right of the screen to do this).

Pull down the **Insert** menu and select **Clipart**.

You will see the Microsoft® Art Gallery which will look similar to this (the first time it will add the clipart for you and you can add any additional clipart by using the **Options** within the Gallery).

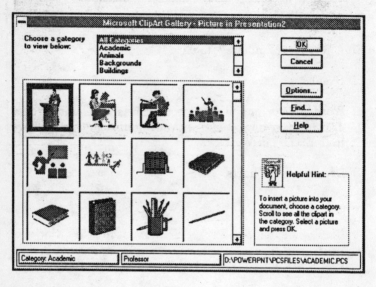

Select the image you want from the library and you will see
it appear within the slide, it can then be altered.

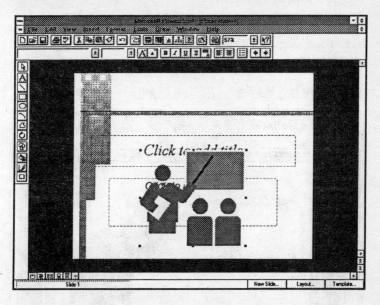

Pictures Or Scanned Images

These are treated in a very similar way to clipart, they can
(mostly but not always, depending upon the type of file) be
sized, recoloured, grouped and ungrouped and so on.

Hints:
- ☐ Scanned images require a large amount of disc space to
  store and tend to slow the system up when used.

- ☐ A partial fix for this is to scale the scanned image before
  saving it so that it is the correct size.

- ☐ However you should not make it too small as increasing
  the size of an image can reduce the definition, just as
  reducing the size of a large image may increase its
  definition (again this will vary with the type of file).

To insert a picture (that is not in the Microsoft® Art Gallery), pull down the **Insert** menu and select **Picture**.

Find the picture by choosing the correct drive and directory and then the file and it will be imported into your presentation.

The screen below shows a picture imported in this way.

A Word for Windows™ Table

This lets you easily create and import a table from Word™.

Pull down the **Insert** menu and choose **Microsoft® Word™ Table**.

The first screen you will see is a dialog box that allows you to choose the number of rows and columns in the table.

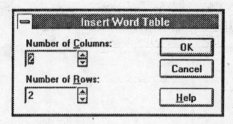

The table will then appear and you can enter whatever you want to within it.

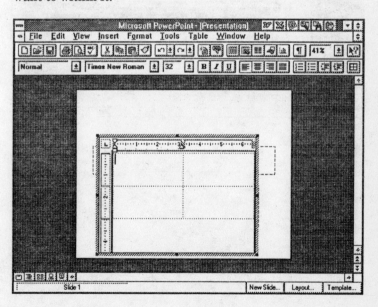

As you can see from the screen below, while you are entering data into the table (or if you have selected and double clicked the table) the Word6 menus are available.

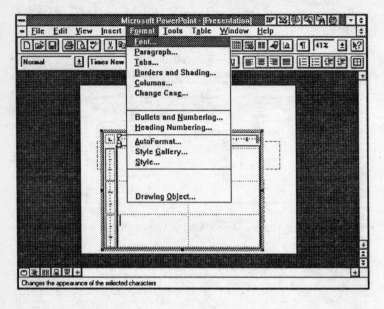

Graphs

You can insert graphs by selecting **Insert** and then **Microsoft® Graph** or by clicking on the toolbar button.

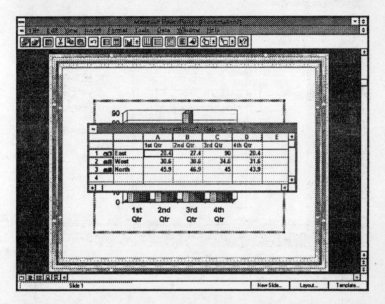

You will see the screen (above), this is **Microsoft® Graph** (a mini application that can be accessed from all the main applications such as PowerPoint™ and Word™).

You can create your own graph by altering and/or adding to the data shown.

Once you start the process you will see some new buttons appear on the toolbar. There are three to the left of the toolbar shown below, these allow you to import data from other files and to view the datasheet. The others deal with the chart itself.

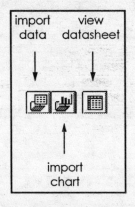

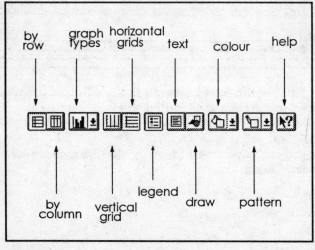

After entering the figures and text into the spreadsheet table, you can choose to improve your graph by using the various buttons and you can add text, etc. Graphs can be sized and so on in a similar way to other visuals.

Here is one I made earlier.

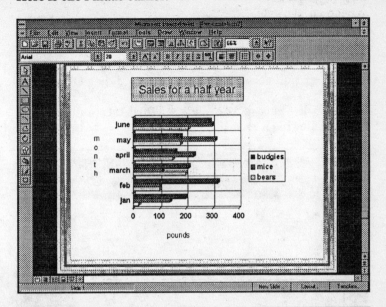

Hint:
- [ ] If you want to import a chart you have already created in Excel™ simply click on the appropriate button on the toolbar.

WordArt™

Another type of object you can insert into your presentation is WordArt™. You can create special text effects by using this.

To start off, pull down the **Insert** menu and then **Object**.

From the list choose **Microsoft® WordArt2** and you will see the following screen.

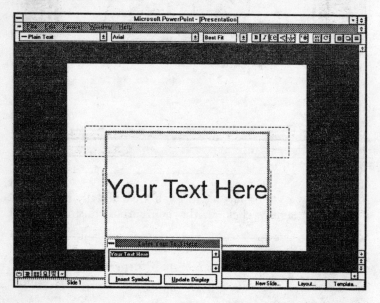

You can type in your text in the box shown and use the buttons that appear on the toolbar to modify the size and appearance of the text.

By experimenting you will be able to build up very sophisticated effects.

A simple example is shown below.

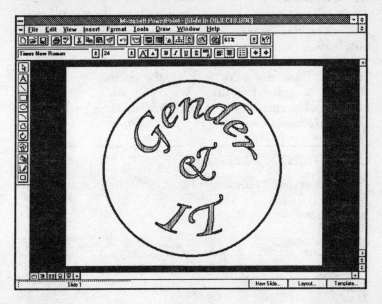

Other Objects

There are several other objects you can add to your presentation, for example **Note-It** (the computer equivalent of sticky labels) and the **Equation Editor** (using this you can enter very complex mathematical symbols and equations).

All the available objects are listed when you insert an object and each has its own **Help** screens to make life easier for you.

Organisation Charts

One of the advantages of a program such as PowerPoint™ is the variety of predesigned diagrams and other graphics available.

Some of these are dealt with in the chapter **Using Sample Layouts**, this section is devoted to organisation charts which is a commonly used feature and is allocated its own button on the toolbar.

Click on this button and you will be presented with the following screen. This is the Microsoft® Organisation Chart screen and can be called up from any of the latest applications.

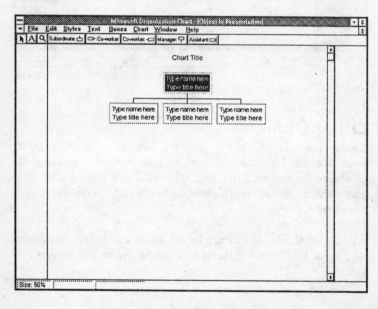

As you can see from the enlarged illustration below, you enter the name and title by highlighting the relevant text and overtyping.

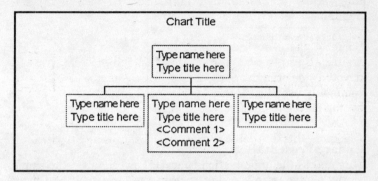

Chart Title

Type name here
Type title here

Type name here
Type title here

Type name here
Type title here
<Comment 1>
<Comment 2>

Type name here
Type title here

Hint:
☐ By clicking again on any box you can add comments which show on the organisation chart

Some of the items on this screen differ from the mainstream menus and are explained below.

File Menu

New...	Ctrl+N
Open...	Ctrl+O
Close	Ctrl+F4
Update Presentation	
Save Copy As...	
Revert...	
Exit and Return to Presentation	

The new commands are :

Update Presentation
This makes the organisation chart in PowerPoint™ the same as the one you are working with in the Organisation Chart screen.

Revert
This discards the changes you have made since the last time you saved the chart.

Edit Menu
The different commands are **Select** and **Select All**. This lets you select boxes within the chart.

Hint:
☐ You can select all or part of the chart by clicking and dragging the mouse over the boxes you want to select.

Styles Menu

This menu show you a series of group styles which you can apply to any boxes within your chart that you have selected.

Group styles:		
ᗡᗡᗡ	⊟⊟	⊟⊟
⊟⊟⊟	⌶	⬜
Assistant		⊡⊥⊡
Co-manager		⊡⊡⊡

Text

Within this menu you can alter the alignment, font or colour of the **selected** text.

Boxes

Similarly you can alter the look of selected boxes by altering the lines, colours, etc.

Chart

This lets you size the chart, change the background colour and display the **Draw** tools so that you can customise your chart.

Help

The organisation chart screen has its own specific help.

Additional Toolbar Buttons

The picture below shows the new buttons found within the Organisation Chart screen.

Add On Symbols

These can be added to any **selected** box to customise the chart to portray the organisational structure you want.

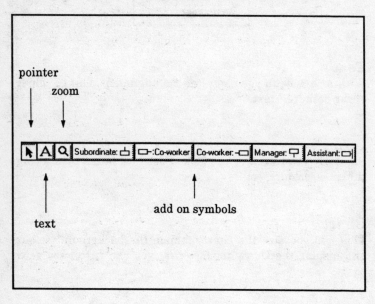

Using Sample Layouts

PowerPoint™ contains several sample layouts which can be used as they exist or altered to your specific needs.

They are found within the **Samples** directory within the PowerPoint™ structure. When you have selected the directory you will see the list of sample layouts.

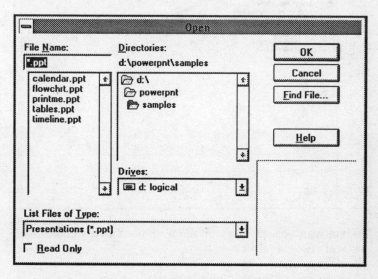

You can choose from a calendar, flowcharts, printme, tables and a timeline. Each of these gives you a choice of different layouts based upon a common theme.

How To Use the Samples

Once you have selected your choice of sample, in this case **Tables**, the first screen you will see is an outline of the slides making up this particular sample file. This is shown below.

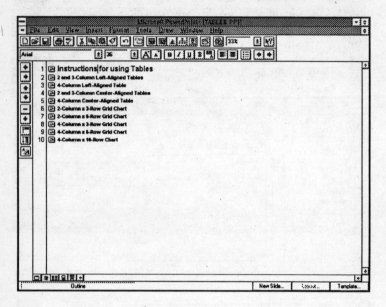

As you can see, this comprises a slide of instructions and several types of table.

Click on any of these to highlight the text and then click on the **Slide View** button to see it full screen.

The instruction slide gives basic information (shown below).

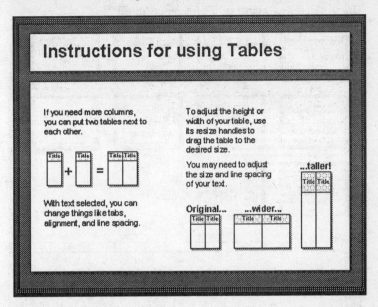

You then choose one of the sample tables, you can scroll through them one by one or use the **Slide Sorter** to display them all at once.

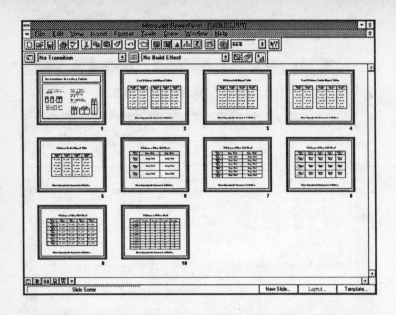

Copying Samples Into Presentations

After choosing the one you want, display it and then pull down the **Edit** menu and **Select All**

Then click on the **Copy** button on the toolbar and finally select the **File** menu and **Close** the sample file.

Now open a new file or select the slide you want the sample to appear within and use the **Paste** button to paste it into the slide.

Now enter the necessary text. Remember that you can alter the font and font size of the text as you wish, you can also add graphics and so on.

Your table (or other sample) is now part of your presentation, save it before you lose your hard work.

Hints:

☐ You can **Ungroup** the table to delete parts of it, copy and paste parts, add lines and graphics as desired to produce a totally customised table.

☐ You can alter and save a table or other sample either as a slide within the sample file or as another sample file so that if you regularly want to use a layout you do not have to re-create it each time.

The other sample layouts are illustrated below.

Calendar

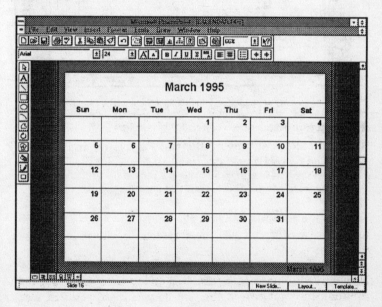

Flow Charts

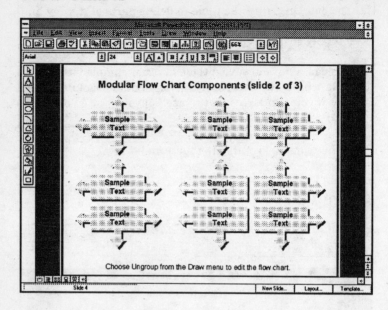

Printme

These are slides displaying the various colours and shading within the PowerPoint™ program.

Timelines

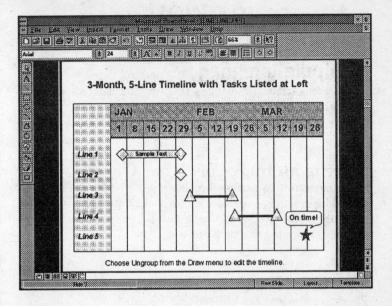

Artwork

Manipulating Images

There are various techniques that can be used to enhance the image (and these techniques can be applied to most visuals and objects of whatever type).

Moving an Image or Other Object

Make sure that the image has been selected (it should have little black squares around it) then click the mouse within the image and *while holding down the mouse button* move the mouse pointer to a new position.

Sizing an Image or Object

There are two ways to achieve this, **either**

☐ Select the image and then position the mouse pointer on one of the small black squares surrounding the image.

☐ The mouse pointer should become a small line with arrows at either end.

☐ While keeping the mouse button held down, move the mouse either in or out to resize the image.

or

☐ Select the image and pull down the **Draw** menu and select **Scale**. You will see a dialog box, all you need to do is to enter the percentage you want to scale to.

Note that you can size relative to the original (which is the default setting and keeps the correct proportions) and scale for the best scale for the slide show to optimise the image for viewing within the slide show.

Cut and Paste
Remember that you can **Cut, Copy and Paste** text or images using the appropriate buttons on the toolbar.

Paste Special
This is similar to the **Paste** command but gives you more control and allows you to create a link to the originating application.

If an object is linked, it will be automatically updated when the original is changed.

Duplicate
This allows you to duplicate a slide so that an identical copy is added to the presentation (next to the original). It works by using the **Slide Sorter View**, selecting the required slide and then pulling down the **Edit** menu and clicking on **Duplicate**.

Delete Slide

By pulling down the **Edit** menu and choosing **Delete Slide**, you can delete the current slide (or the selected slide(s) in Slide Sorter View).

You can also delete a slide in **Slide Sorter View** by selecting the slide(s) and then pressing the **Del** key.

Hint:
☐ You can use the **Undo** button if you quickly realise you have deleted the slide(s) accidentally.

Links

You can edit a linked object by using the **Edit** menu or much more simply by **double clicking** the mouse on the object.

Either method loads the originating application and the object within it, you make the necessary changes and **Exit** back to PowerPoint™.

Objects

You can edit objects by using the **Edit** menu followed by **Objects** or more quickly by **double clicking** the mouse on the object.

You may be asked if you want to convert it to a PowerPoint™ object. This will ungroup it and has the same effect as using the **Draw** and **Ungroup** commands.

Cropping an Object

Cropping is different from sizing, sizing makes the whole image smaller (or bigger), when you crop an object you remove part of the whole object.

This is sometimes useful to remove extraneous parts of a picture or other image.

To do this use the **Tools** menu and select **Crop Picture**. A little cropping tool will appear.

You then grab any corner of your object with the tool and take out the bits you want to.

Hint:
☐ You can bring back any part of a cropped image in the same way you removed it.

Here are two images, one before cropping and one after.

To achieve this I copied the original image then cropped each to leave the faces, then some of the second image had to be recoloured to remove part of the image by making it white.

Altering Colours

Select the image and then pull down the **Tools** menu and select **Recolor**.

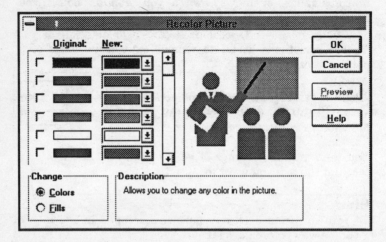

You can change any of the original colours to any other colour and by clicking on the **Preview** button you can see the effect before committing yourself.

It is possible to revert back to the original colours by removing the X from the side of any of the Original colour boxes.

Grouping and Ungrouping

You may want to use only a part of an image or you may want to rearrange the component parts of it.

To do this select the image and then pull down the **Draw** menu and then choose **Ungroup**.

A message may appear on the screen which you can (if you want to ungroup the image) agree to.

You will see that the image is now made up of many sub-images all identified by the little black squares surrounding them.

Click outside the image and then click on any component and you can move it, recolour it, size it or delete it as you wish.

Hint:
☐ To select more than one component or object hold down the **Shift** key while clicking the mouse on each item you want to select.

The illustration shows the images moved away from each other.

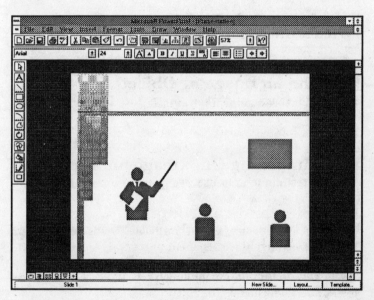

When you want to merge several images or objects into one so that they form a single group which can be moved or resized as a single item, you can do this in several ways.

☐ Hold down the mouse button and drag the mouse around the items. This will select all the items.

or

☐ While holding down the **shift** key, click the mouse on each item you want to include within the group.

or

☐ Pull down the **Edit** menu and choose **Select All**.

Then (whichever method is used) pull down the **Draw** menu and choose **Group** or **Regroup** from the menu.

Deleting an Image or Object
Select the image and then press the **Del** key on the keyboard.

Superimposing One Image on Another
A useful technique is to use two or more images to create a new one.

Insert the two images and carry out any sizing, ungrouping or sizing you wish to.

Select one of the images and move it physically over the other.

Below is an example of two images used together, the original one was ungrouped, one part deleted and the components moved around, the blackboard was recoloured. The second image, the donkey, was sized and then moved onto the blackboard.

Rotate/Flip Objects

You can rotate or flip objects within PowerPoint™. To do so, select the **Draw** menu and select **Rotate/Flip**. You will be given the following choices.

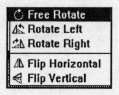

Free Rotate lets you grab any of the corners with the rotate tool and rotate to your heart's desire.

Below is an example.

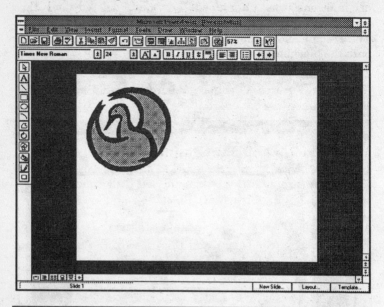

Hint:
☐ If your image will not allow you to choose **Rotate/Flip**
then if you **Ungroup** it (**Draw** menu) and then **Group** it
again, it becomes a PowerPoint™ object and can be
rotated.

Adding Borders and Arrows

You can add borders or arrows anywhere within your presentation, they can be used for text and objects.

Borders

There are two ways to achieve a border around an object or text.

Using the text/object boundaries

Click on the object or text so that the text box or object boundaries are shown (you should see little black squares positioned around the border).

Then pull down the **Format** menu and select **Colours & Lines**. Choose the colour and thickness of the line and so on.

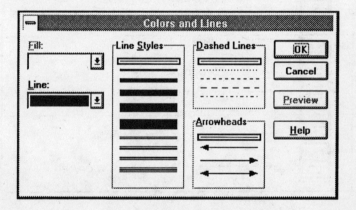

Creating your own border

Use the **Border Tool** (drawing toolbar) to create the border then pull down the **Format** menu and select **Colours & Lines** and so on.

Arrows/Lines

Use the line draw tool (Draw toolbar) and then after selecting the line pull down the **Format** menu and select **Colours & Lines**. Choose the arrow and so on.

Creating and Manipulating Shapes and Pictures

You can create your own images, boxes and so on using the drawing toolbar.

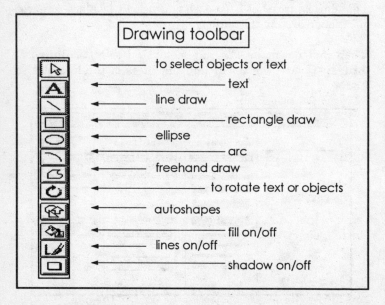

Drawing toolbar

- to select objects or text
- text
- line draw
- rectangle draw
- ellipse
- arc
- freehand draw
- to rotate text or objects
- autoshapes
- fill on/off
- lines on/off
- shadow on/off

To do this simply select the appropriate tool by clicking on it and create the object you want by pressing the left hand mouse button where you want to start and letting go of the button when finished.

You have created an object and just like any other object this can be selected by clicking on it and it can then be moved or deleted and so on.

The Draw Menu

The **Draw** menu also gives you some control over the use of objects.

Some of these have been dealt with earlier in the chapter; the ways the remainder may be used are described below.

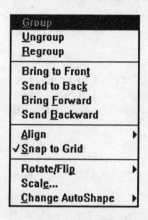

Arranging Superimposed Objects

You may want to place one object on top of another, the order in which these can be displayed can be critical to the result.

Think of the objects as being stacked, one on top of the next. The commands to vary the sequence are :

Bring to Front

This brings the selected object to the front of the pile.

Send to Back

This sends the selected object to the back of the pile.

Bring Forward

This brings the selected object forward one level in the pile.

Send Backward

This sends the selected object back one level in the pile.

Align

This is used to align objects and/or text, you have to have selected more than one object or text for this to be usable, then simply pull down the **Draw** menu and **Align**. You have a choice of alignments and you can experiment with this technique.

Hints:

☐ To select more than one item hold down the **Shift** key while clicking the items.

☐ Save the file **before** making any experimental changes to it.

Snap to Grid

There is an (invisible) grid and any object or text aligns itself to this. It makes lining up easier to achieve but does reduce fine control.

You can turn the **Snap to Grid** feature on or off by selecting it (**Draw** and then **Snap to Grid**). If it is active, there will be a tick.

Change Autoshape

Autoshapes are the various shapes you can use within your presentation.

By clicking on the **Autoshape** button in the **Drawing Toolbar** you will have a selection of shapes.

Click on the shape you want to use and then click within the slide to create it by dragging the mouse. An object using this shape will be created and like any other object it can be sized, moved, recoloured and so on.

Change Autoshape allows you to select any shape (it does not have to be created by using **Autoshapes** but could be a box or ellipse) and then after pulling down the **Draw** menu and **Change Autoshapes** you can select any other shape to replace the original shape.

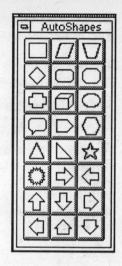

Adding Shadow

In a similar way to lines/borders, select the line/object/border and using the **Format** menu select **Shadow**. Choose the shadow and offset (degree of shadow) and you have a shadow effect.

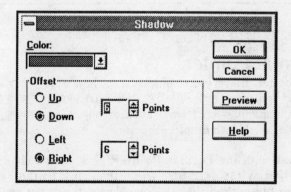

Again you can **Preview** the effect before committing yourself.

Below you can see an illustration of the effect together with the **Autoshapes** toolbar.

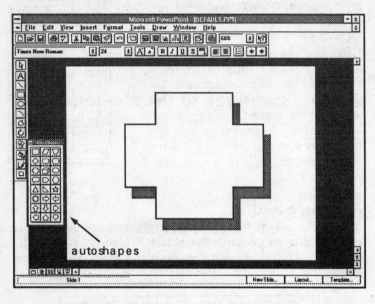

autoshapes

Format Painter

This button allows you to quickly alter how any object appears by copying the attributes (colour, shading, etc.) from another object (it does not work with graphs or pictures).

To work with the **Format Painter**, click on the object you want to copy the attributes **from**, then click on the Format Painter button and then on the object you want to copy the attributes to.

Altering Your Slides

Some of the ways of altering your slides have already been covered, for example changing the template, this chapter deals with the various other methods of customising the look of your presentation so that it stands out from the clones.

Making Changes to the Master Slide

You can alter individual slides or you can make global changes to all the slides by amending the **Master** slide.

To do this pull down the **View** menu and select **Master**. You will be able to choose which type of master you alter from the list shown below.

Slide Master
Outline Master
Handout Master
Notes Master

You will then see the **Master** appear and any changes or additions you make to this will be reflected in the master you have altered and all the slides making up the presentation.

Below is an example of a master slide with the date added and moved to the bottom left of the slide. See how the date is shown as two lines, this means that it will be the date the file is printed or displayed, not the day it was created.

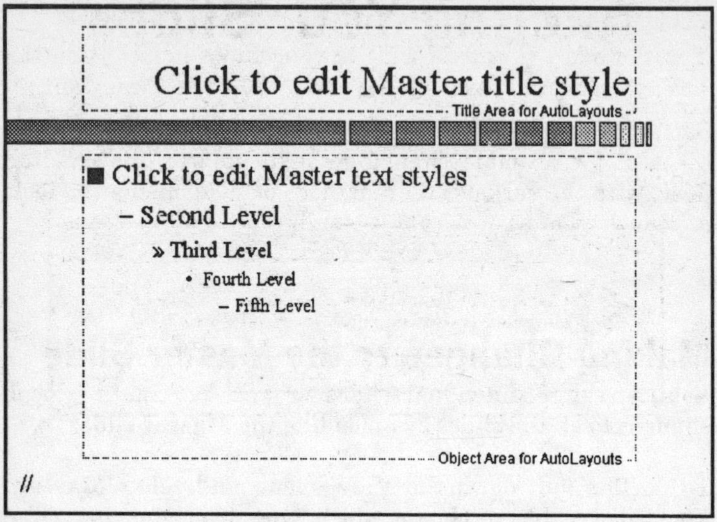

Deleting Slides

This can be achieved in two ways.

☐ In **Slide Sorter** view select the slide or slides by clicking on them and press the **Delete** key.

☐ In **Slide View** pull down the **Edit** menu and then select **Delete**.

Hint:
☐ To select more than one slide hold down the **Shift** key while clicking the mouse on each slide you want to select.

Adding a Timescale to Your Slides

You can add the date or time to your slides by selecting the **Insert** menu and choosing the particular option you want.

Note that you have to enter this onto the **Master** not on individual slides as you can see from the dialog box shown.

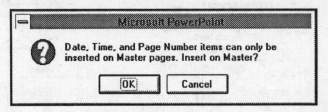

Adding Page Numbers

This works the same way as adding the date or time.

Hint:
☐ You can alter the font and size of the date, time or page numbers and move them anywhere within the master slide.

Altering the Slide Background

Pull down the **Format** menu and select **Slide Background**.
You will see the following dialog box.

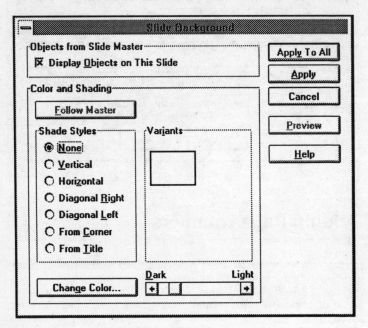

You can experiment with the various shadings and pick from the variations thereon.

One of the useful features of much of PowerPoint™ is being able to **Preview** the changes before committing yourself.

Below is an example of the shading applied to a plain slide.

Be careful with the buttons **Apply To All** and **Apply**. Your choice will depend upon whether you want to change the background of all the slides or not.

Changing the Colour Schemes

This operates in a similar way to changing the backgrounds,
however there is no preview button, you will see any changes
in the bottom left of the dialog box.

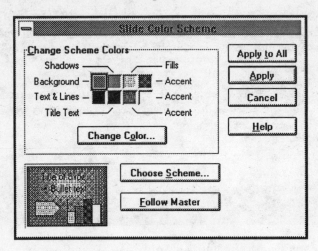

Slide Setup

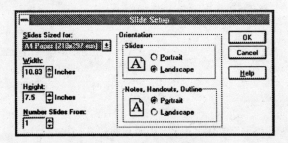

It is best to set this for your default slide show, you are most
likely to want to alter the paper size.

Inserting Slides from Another File

This option lets you add slides from another file into your current presentation.

To do this pull down the **Insert** menu and select **Slides from File**. You will see a dialog box similar to the Open File dialog box and you simply select the file you want to add.

Note that the new slides will be added after the current slide, and the other slides in the original presentation will be re-sequenced.

> **Hint:**
> ☐ You may find it best to use **Slide Sorter View** and position the cursor where you want the new slides to be added.

Inserting Slides from an Outline

This is slightly different in that PowerPoint™ will automatically create a slide show from an outline, using the outline levels as a guide, the first level text is treated as a heading and so on.

For example if you either created an outline within **Word for Windows**™ or used an outline from an existing file then you could use this to create a PowerPoint™ presentation without having to retype the text.

This works rather effectively and is a real time-saver.

To do this pull down the **Insert** menu and select **Slides from Outline**. Find the file you want to use and PowerPoint™ will convert it into a presentation. You will then need to make any alterations and to customise the presentation.

Customising the Program

Like all Microsoft® programs, PowerPoint™ has various customisation features.

Customise the Toolbars

This enables you to alter the toolbars by adding and deleting toolbars and the associated buttons to reflect the way you personally work.

Adding or Removing Toolbars

You can add or remove any of a number of different toolbars to your screen.

To do this pull down the **View** menu and select **Toolbars**. You will see the dialog box shown below.

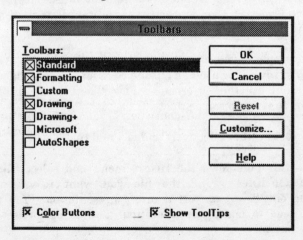

By selecting or deselecting the different toolbars you can add (or remove) them.

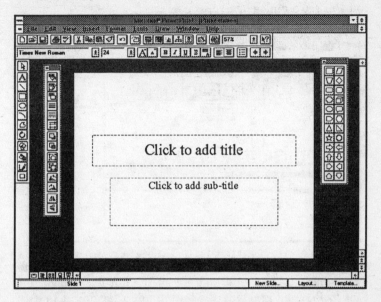

Above is a screen where several additional toolbars have been added.

Hints :
- [ ] You can select a toolbar on the screen by double-clicking on it, you can then move it around the screen to a new position.

- [ ] Once a toolbar has been selected you can change the shape by moving the mouse pointer along an edge until it becomes a two headed arrow which can then be dragged to produce a new shape.

Customising a Toolbar

After pulling down the **Tools** menu, select **Customise** and you will see a dialog box.

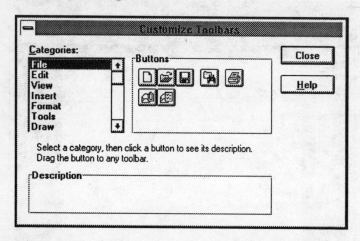

You can select from the different toolbars shown in the **Categories** column and add any of the buttons shown (for that toolbar) by grabbing the button and dragging it to **any** toolbar on the screen.

Likewise to remove any button from a toolbar on the screen simply drag the button away from the toolbar while the **Customise Toolbar** dialog box is shown.

Hint:
☐ If you decide that you have made a mess of any toolbar then the **Reset** button on the **Toolbar** menu (**View**) lets you put everything back to its previous position.

Options

Also in the **Tools** menu is **Options**. This is where you can make various choices as shown in the dialog box and explained where necessary below.

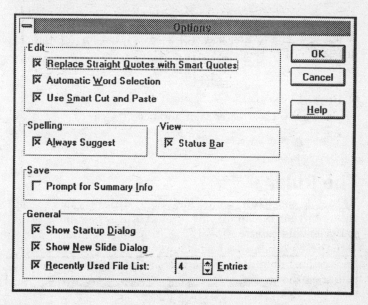

Replace Straight Quotes with Smart Quotes
Alters ordinary quotes (straight quotes) with curly ones which you may prefer.

Automatic Word Selection
When you use the mouse to select text, the text is highlighted in groups of words, if this feature is turned off then you will be able to select partial words or individual characters.

Smart Cut and Paste
Makes spaces between words when the Clipboard contents are pasted into your slides.

Always Suggest
When you use the spell checker, it will always suggest alternative words.

Prompt for Summary Info
When you save a file, you will be prompted for information unless you turn this off.

General
You can show these screens or not as you wish.

The Ruler
By using the **View** menu and then **Rulers** you can add rulers to your screen display. Select **Rulers** again to revert to not having rulers.

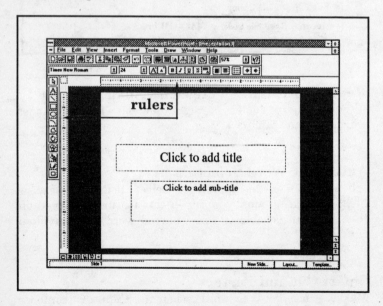

The rulers are useful if you want to position or size objects precisely. See how, when using rulers, the position of the mouse is shown on each ruler.

Guides

Similarly you can display or hide the guides by using the **View** menu and then **Guides**.

Guides are useful to position objects or text and they can be moved horizontally or vertically by clicking the mouse pointer on the guide and dragging it.

The Help Screens

As with all Windows programs the on-line **Help** screens are a valuable and easy to use feature of the program and make both learning and problem solving easier.

The Help menu is shown below.

Contents
Search for Help on...
Index
Quick Preview
Ti**p** of the Day...
C**u**e Cards
Technical Support
About Microsoft PowerPoint...

Hint:
☐ Pressing the function key **F1** will bring up relevant help within any part of the program.

Contents

This is a list of the topics available, as shown below.

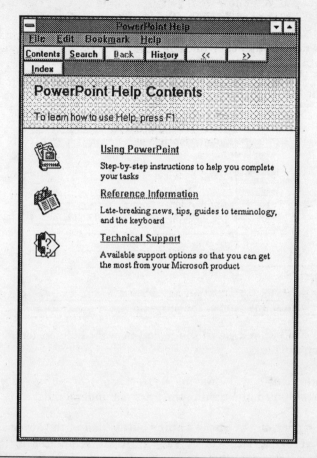

Hint:

☐ Windows™ Help screens use two types of green type. If you click on the type with full underlining a screen explaining that topic will appear and so on until you get the information you want. Dotted underlining means that if you click on the words then you will see a box explaining the word or concept.

Search for Help on

As long as you know what you are looking for then this is the fastest method of obtaining the necessary guidance.

You will see the following screen.

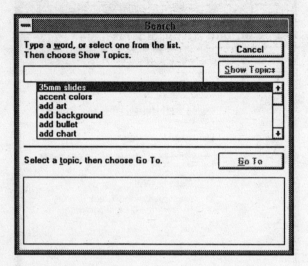

You can either type in the topic you want help on (or scroll down the list).

PowerPoint™ will find the nearest word or phrase if you haven't typed in anything the program understands.

Then click on the **Show Topics** button and in the lower half of the dialog box will be shown all the references to that topic. You select the one you want and click on the **Go To** button and there you are.

Index

This is a quick way of navigating around the Help screens. You can click on the first letter of your word and then the topics beginning with that letter will be shown. You may need to scroll down the screen to see them all.

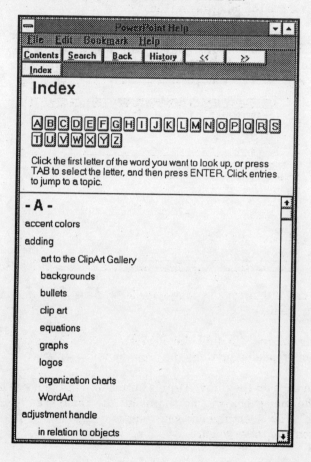

Quick Preview

Gives an overview of the main features of the program.

Tip of the Day

This option enables you to see all the daily tips together and it is worthwhile looking through them periodically as they contain all sorts of useful information which will save you time and enhance your presentations.

Cue Cards

These literally coach you through various activities within PowerPoint™ and are a great help if you are learning or use the program infrequently. The list of things you can do is shown below.

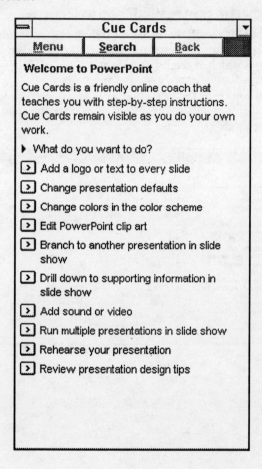

Technical Support

Information on how to obtain support from Microsoft®.

About Microsoft® PowerPoint™

This tells you about the version of the program and has an option to display a screen of data about your system, an example of which is displayed below.

This may not be as technically useful as say Norton Utilities, but does give some information and statistics about your current system.

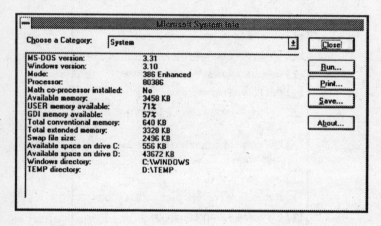

Coping with Presentations

First Things

Decide **WHAT** you want to achieve.

☐ Do you want to impart factual information or to persuade your audience in some way (e.g. to change their beliefs or attitudes).

☐ Decide upon the type of audience you are addressing, what do they want from the presentation, pitch the level of your presentation carefully, audiences vary in their attention span, intellectual ability, etc.

☐ Decide upon the best way to get your message across for the specific audience you are presenting to.

The Material

Write down the main points you want to make and then underneath each main point write the detail. An outliner is a very useful tool for this.

The audience likes to have something to take away, so prepare a handout or copy of the OHPs you have used, you can reduce the OHPs so that up to six can be printed onto one page of handout (see the chapter on **Output**).

The Presentation

Always introduce the material and yourself to the audience and remember to wrap it all up at the end by summarising what you have told them.

Funny (short) stories that are **relevant** help enormously in retaining the audience's attention.

Your voice is of primary importance, keep it slow and interested, emphasise the important points and the changes of topic, this keeps your audience awake.

Always try to maintain eye contact with as many of the audience as possible, this is easiest if you are familiar with your material and do not need to use cue cards to any extent.

Always practise, preferably in front of a live audience or video camera (the first time you see a video of yourself can be traumatic, it is almost as though a stranger is facing you).

The audience is most likely to have a worthwhile experience if you exude enthusiasm, seem to be enjoying yourself and appear to know your subject.

The Environment Itself

Always check the room, seating, lighting and the display equipment (computer, OHP, LCD, etc.) **well before** the actual presentation.

Make sure that all the audience can actually see the screen easily (try not to stand in front of it). Arrange the seating as necessary and adjust any other environmental features (heating, lighting, etc.) to maximise the effect.

Using Software

Keep a consistent style throughout the slides, if you are using templates maintain the same one throughout each section of the presentation if not through all of it.

Use clipart, charts or drawings to make points or to amuse but be careful not to detract from the actual message. Using a logo on every slide helps maintain a corporate image. Under no circumstances overdo the use of clipart or other graphics.

Keep the slides as simple as possible, too much detail is pointless and counter-productive, the purpose of the slides is to emphasise the main points of your talk **not** to replace the talk itself.

Use initial capital letters but then lower case (i.e. not all capitals).

Keep the number of words, lines, numbers or graphic images to the absolute minimum for each slide (the maximum number of lines should not be more than six).

Make sensible use of fonts and remember that you need to use fairly large fonts so that the audience can read them easily without effort. It is likely that font sizes less than 18 points will not be readable, in many cases the larger the text the more effective it will be.

You may also like to consider the following:

☐ Creating a professional finish by ending with a blank coloured slide or a slide with your company logo. This also works well between sections of a presentation

☐ You can press the B character on the keyboard to blank the screen during presentations.

☐ Use the **rehearsal** feature to time your slide show (**View, Slide Show** and then **Rehearse New Timings**). As a start work on the principle that each slide will take around three minutes (although this will vary on the content and how long you talk about it).

Colours and Things

Be careful with your use of colour (or shades of grey). Also:

☐ Try to avoid complicated images or backgrounds as these can be confusing to the audience and detract from the points you are trying to put across.

☐ Be aware of contrasts, for OHPs dark letters on a light backdrop show up well, charts and diagrams also look good with a light (but not too bright) background. However for 35mm slides a dark background and light text may work best.

☐ Do not overdo the number or variety of colours or grey shades on any slide and remember that different colours affect the audience in different ways.

Index